A FURTHER EXILE

A Further Exile

Tom Henihan

Ekstasis  Editions

National Library of Canada Cataloguing in Publication Data

Henihan, Tom
    A further exile

    Poems.
    ISBN 1-894800-04-4

    I. Title.
PS8565.E5824F87 2002   C811'.54   C2002-910333-9
PR9199.3.H452F87 2002

© Tom Henihan, 2002.
Cover Art: Bruce McMahon

Published in 2002 by:
Ekstasis Editions Canada Ltd.   Ekstasis Editions
Box 8474, Main Postal Outlet   Box 571
Victoria, B.C. V8W 3S1   Banff, Alberta T0L 0C0

THE CANADA COUNCIL | LE CONSEIL DES ARTS
FOR THE ARTS | DU CANADA
SINCE 1957 | DEPUIS 1957

BRITISH
COLUMBIA
ARTS COUNCIL
Supported by the Province of British Columbia

A Further Exile has been published with the assistance of a grant from the Canada Council and the Cultural Services Branch of British Columbia.

For Monica

CONTENTS

ABSENCE

The closest we get to belonging is yearning to belong
until finally like a thorn at the edge of a star
we give everything we possess to the cold
and take that feral hand of the river
where it reaches the sea.

Some element of myself has fallen away
and the world seems so large now
with this distance that rests between us.
The stone face of my prayer is unable to penetrate the void
with its profile of clay and fire.

What can I do with all these moments that are left to me?
With the white sheets of the afternoon.
With the nights that are still palpable
with the warm milk of your body
and the scent of your hair sultry with illness.

In every room of this house
the doors open on a strange new undertaking
and the dust of your absence lingers about me
like sins without ownership.

The Luminous Void

In every strand of light
I see the coast of a dream
you had to abandon.
Walking there
in that luminous void
pulls me closer to the touch
of your vital hands
that swim in the light
with your concise approach.

And now that you are unfettered
by the chains of dark water
that cling to the earth
you cannot open your arms anymore
to the adventure
of our old attachments.
However, I continue to love
the immeasurable night
though I know
it can give me no comfort.

You seemed to know
how to absorb
the gentle urgency of the breeze
when it became endowed
with the aloof aspect of winter.
You never considered
crying out to the sleeping centuries
when they aimed their weapons
at the stars above your house.

Did you envision the end
as a fleet of translucent ships
floating in the mist
wounding themselves against every wave.

Did you see that consummate moment
devour itself in an emblem of smoke.
Did you see yourself
scrutinising the enigma
of the curving light above the water
while listening
to the unharnessed ropes of the wind
beating the world.

In the Harsh Light

Those numbered days were so fragile
under the harsh tropical light.
I feel now that I should
have spoken with you
and held you more often
but that world was so distant and faded
with fierce light
it wouldn't yield anything to me.

It was sad to watch you
being brave about dying
and I wondered was it because
you were being watched.
And I thought why pretend at courage
when the world itself trembles
like keys in your pocket
like foreign change from a voyage
that steals everything from you.

Through those nights
above my sleep there extended
from the marble shadows cool as water
a nostalgic terrace
that hosted your naked arms
and your fragrant summer dress
and beyond the terrace
a street with strange trees
that prepared me
for the homelessness I now feel.

My world has changed forever
and the only resolution
is acceptance.
Constantly now
something arrives and departs within me
something from far away that I know intimately . ..
the feeling of rising up and being lost.

THE FIRST AUTUMN

This season owns me.
The light gives the mountains
a cathedral countenance.
The world without you is a bell
swaying in that jaded light.
Your graceful presence is with me now
it comes to me as a voice over a lake
when the air is heavy with cold perfume.
At this time of year
I loved to watch you tend
the last brittle threads
of the flowers we had planted
when the soil was shiny, dark and promising.
The little stone wall we arranged in the garden
looks old and monumental
though it is only one year since we built it.
This season that is coming is terrible.
The rest of the world has gone indoors.

Sometimes It Is

It is as impossible
as touching the night
touching the idea
that all I can do now
is remember you.
Sometimes it is
a familiar landscape
cast in a beguiling light
that makes
losing you unbearable.
Sometimes it is
a stormy and beautiful sky
that comes to burden me
with the gentle things
that happened
while I was looking
the other way.

A Leaf and its Shadow

The tender nails of the rain
seize the earth
while the gate to every house
swings with a lament
that badgers our bones
with a blue telegram of mist.
And though we know
that it doesn't matter
if we have
the courage for it or not
because it is inevitable
that we will enter
that hermitage
of sleep and grass.
Yet the things our hands
conceal from the world
are the things
we hold most intimate
especially the
barbarous riverbed
of our crisis
and the sky of famine
and sleeping animals
that we pull over ourselves
at dawn.
And though we know
sometimes we forget
that every kindness
is a wounded bird
carrying a leaf
and its shadow
and that sometimes
we just cry
to dampen the obvious
so we can knead the world

into love and hate.
And because we know
and forget so much
we salt and dry our time
into a contingency
that is never called upon
while we continue to kiss
our own conceited pain
as though it were a toad
wearing a crown.

CRUEL ANGEL

The colours of the sky
are faded
with a potent apathy.
It is the gown
of a cruel angel
who governs the house
while sleeping.
It is strange
how her kingdom
of bleached light
turns us
to hungry children
who curb our breath
though we want to cry
with the rattle
of the dry grass
and the redolence
of the earth.

Bow Valley

An enormous evening
is dying magnificently
over the mountains.
The white skulls of animals
emulate the sky
by flourishing
inside their own dreams
until they are completely lost.
The wind comes and goes
confused as a bird's
first moment of freedom.
The trees waltz
in each others arms
with the ardour of children
at a boisterous wedding.
The river yields to the world
its branches of dark water
while the evening moans
from the depths of its dominion
as it descends the ladder
of its own blood
and enters the clay
that has eaten
the veins of the sky.

An Invisible Wheel

Impetuous as blood
the sky digresses
at the frontier of the world.
As it transfigures itself
it illuminates vaguely
our tenuous encounters
and fateful departures.
The murmuring urge of the wind
incites the poignant light.
Gladly the sound
of the river intrudes
as it turns
with its dark shoulders
an invisible wheel.
The horses' nostrils tremble
at the essence of oblivion.
Their eyes are deep
with the hard ebony
of the urban night
but they know the futility
of grazing among crystal
and liquid gold.
They favour the dawn
with her breasts at ease
in the flagging grass
and her tongue of damp light
sousing the hills.

BADLANDS

There is an antediluvian grandeur
and the imminence of fire in the sky.
A hawk, fastidious as a soldier
single-minded as a warrior
crosses above the badlands.
Neither hunger nor the heat of conflict
distract it from its own cardinal rule.
A snake, venomous and electric
transcribes its story in the dust
between the brittle grass.
Striking out from a small lake
the reflected light crosses swords
before a curtain of preliminary darkness.

PAST AND PRESENT

Time is eating the air around me
and though I have nothing
every moment
I feel something of value
fall away from me.
There are paths I took long ago
that I now see fading towards me
along the evening sky.
The past haunts me
the prescribed one
the one that never came to pass.
It is an apparition that sits
at the opposite side of my table.
It is a stubborn candle of straw
put out by the rain.
The wind that rattles my window
knows only of fury, thirst
and things that are insatiable.
One side of its cloak
wants to be water
the other wants to be stone.
It sweeps through the world
with a despairing charity
relentlessly searching
for its own gifts.

A Further Exile

This house needs a storm.
Its walls sustain a cruel repose.
Its rituals have lost their rhythm.
Its food is consumed
at an indifferent table.
Why do I aspire to safe places
that stifle me
when I know that my hands
are endowed with bridges
and that I must always return
to the weather and the shattered light.
All I want to do
is to push out to a further exile
to another hill
lit by the moon and a band of snow.
I want to be there
when the wind places its statues of bone
on its altar of silver.
I want something new again.
I want harder light and clearer water.
I want a world that rattles with trains
and nights that remain enamoured with ships.
I want to walk all night
feeling the import of my own story.
I want to walk all night
along the edge of the highway
through the cold vaporous lights
where the drifting snow seems happiest.
Past the trucks that snooze like buffalo.
I want to walk all night
until I can see
with the remoteness of eyes
that have been forced to travel
my own likeness in the morning smoke
that drifts above the fields.

LEAVES AND DUST

In this frenzied hour
of leaves and dust
circling my house
my heart yields
like a flat stone
to a religious holiday.
As in a doomed love affair
I must now embrace
the compelling loneliness
of light invaded by light.
So many roads converge
on the extinguished fire
of the mat inside my door
that I can feel
the seige of the past
throbbing in my arms
asking for order.
So many skies
are folded and draped
over the slow procession
of this hour
that lingers like sleep
that has been induced.

MERCIES

The rain falls gently
while the philandering breeze
waves its branches
between the folds of neighbouring seasons.
Why do I treat these things
as such great mercies?
For me nothing grows cold in the wind
and the faint lights in the distance
shine only on my burden of time.
How the ones I love betray me
when the crystal highways that leave their eyes
bend those distant lights with treachery.
How the ones I love intrigue me
as their faces turn away like ships.
Why do I have to wrestle with each day
in a ritual of phosphorescence
and wounds stained with tea.
Why must I wait all night
for the night itself to grow indifferent
to slip behind the lines and steal some sleep.
The branches beat the distant light
as the rain falls gently
on the black flame of the agitated shadows.

INITIATION

If I could have said good-bye
I would have had no reason to leave.
That night, pivotal as a guiding dream
I tied the distance that lay between us
to the dark boundless element
beneath the wet streets.
Though the wind had its two hands
laden with memories
it whispered "you are not from here"
while an avalanche of local musk
buried every doorway.
Walking towards nothing but the sky
the on-coming night plundered my heart
with teeth of water.
I could see that time was a nail
driven into the air
on which hangs a thread of desire.
So I kissed the air
and hung a light of yellow bread
at my side.

FUGITIVES

The day mounts the hill
of its own scruples
unafraid of what it is becoming

I feel the shadow of an old prayer
on my lips
like a cable of moonlight riding the waves

I let the forsaken blueness of the moment
lean exalted
against the temporal purple of my blood

Some physical wisdom gives my wounds
a reprieve
like fugitives that will run with me tomorrow

NIGHT DRIVING

Through the mist that is rising over the rivers
in the cold that catches their spirit
as they try to escape the harshness of flowing
this voyage of agony sent from the north.
The bridges and lights have their fever.
The highway is smooth and shining with terror,
losing itself in the fray, in circular planets
that live in the blueness of ink.
The earth is the shell of a primordial bird
speckled with beauty,
reddened with its struggle for colour,
containing the profile of water
in the aching stillness of timber
and the silence of stone.
Back towards the mountains in the mind's other darkness
the ice and the animals contend
for the ivory teeth of a dream that has perished.

CLAY

You exist so buoyantly when you dream
like the shift of light on water
but you brood your way
into the weight of your body.
Your life is balanced
on an axle of pure light
where everything breathes
even the shiny metal of the soul
with its ponderous clouds
of feathers and dark honey.
The frontier of your world is a blade
whose sharp edge is a stifled cry
rooted in a handle of clay.

GREEN FLAME

The way the wood gathers time
in its gentle greenness
a spirit of waiting and dying
that lives like a flame.
The sky white as my bones
rests above the trees
where small agonies
of rose and violet
like a storm of nerves
pull in from the sea.
Leaving here won't stop the sky
or becoming a new man
sequestered in the red desert
won't save me from wrestling
with my own green flame
through these afternoons
when desire has left me.
My life is lived
ten paces from itself
in a camouflage of dust
and the odour of invisible animals.
The bone white sky
is too great to take inside
so I must surrender
the way the river
surrenders into its own body
feeling the world
through it own momentum
through the grass and the clay
that define it.

An Immense Heart

Ceremonies inflame every estuary
with the boundless eyes of dangerous gods.
The territory surrounding those eyes
is filled with an unfamiliar darkness
seething with the sweat of enmity
and a pageantry of teeth and bleached bones.

A drum beats with the virtuosity of an immense heart.
The air is moist and fateful as inherited sin.
Fires burn in every hand
sparked from a buried but limitless world,
a world that rests solitary
along the coast of a stone blade.

Led by vibrating footsteps
you locate in the incessant music
a spiral of your own blood
that touches the earth and the sky.
Fragrant dreams are aroused
as the night opens like a heavy dark flower.

The morning comes with a chaste breeze.
A fabulous sky frail as a blue cup
empties itself over the vast fields.
The trees sway
counting time on beads of cold fruit
that they lose in the jagged grass.

INHABITING THE SHADOWS

The dawn shakes its rattle
of muted pollen
over the prone butterflies
and the hornets'
catacomb of vain fantasy
that stole the sky
from yesterday's violets.
Between the leaves and nakedness
where God has spoken
a wealth of grass
blessed by the saliva of animals
and the ritual games of children
inhabits the shadows.
On the bark of trees
crocodiles of brown light sleep.
Here dreams enter the mouth
like dark light
in the chamber of a well.
Eyes the colour of resin and ash
weave through the pure
circumference of hunger
a web of nerves
that are ferocious and shy.
Birds, their colours still wet
with the firmament
their eyes still frightened
with initiation
veil their nests in a liturgy of rain.
In the rich odour
of things growing and dying
the wetness of birth,
the badges of death
on the virgin earth,
the smell of rain
on the skin of the world,

a mystery flowers
in a fountain of branches
in the leaves of blood
beneath the flesh of a child.
Dawn shakes its rattle,
a hand of clay beats time
anticipating the harshness of noon
along the perimeter.

NEBULA

How the world
remains so composed
as it turns in the nebula
of darkness and light
an emblem of yearning
that waits for some word

And how we try to heed
the signs that haunt us
the drift of our blood
the arduous road
that bewitches our hunger
and our obscure days
that scuff the flesh
from the white bone
of the sky

And how the things we want
and the things
we want to relinquish
continue to wrestle
in an emotion of water
until gradually life is lived
through a fragrant appetite
that pulls in the night

REFUGE

There is a hint of the night on her coat
and a snow covered fountain
in the coffee cup
that she waits to be filled.
Though uneasy about the lustre
that escapes from her fingertips
she is glad to be home
and wishes to be catered to and kissed.
A stifled omen sleeps about her lips.
Above the concealed light of her breasts
shadows from the river
hang about her neck and in her hair
and her eyes have amber secrets
that she hopes everyone
will be kind enough not to touch.

ASYLUM

She lives in a territory
of aching shadows
that submerge the borders
of each day.
She locates her source
in the oil of stained tears
and the salve
of her own languid voice.
She sustains a strange repose
remaining silent
as a haunted house.
People just intrude and leave.
Her visage is uncertain
waiting for fulfilment
and though it carries the mark
of all those who defected
it is blessed
with a distant light.
She is perfectly attached
to the gentleness
of her own hands.
The yellow wax of her memory
exhales a flame
that holds a blue sabre.
It makes all monuments look vulgar.
When she dreams
it is the fluid emblems
the things that are concealed
and the wisps of smoke
that endure.

THE RAVINE

A dense odour rises from the ravine.
It is an impenetrable tranquility that holds itself in the air.
It is a languid sacrament consumed with trepidation.
It is a self-inflicted wound bleeding at the centre of it own essence.
Perhaps it is also the effort of the soul to mount the hill of this afternoon
which is hooked on the solitary stem behind this odour.
One could regard the scent as the interval between each embrace
or the arduous tract between our hands
as we wave across some cruel and decisive chasm.

THE INDIGENOUS SHADOWS

The streets sweeten
the crimson medallions
of romance
with the foreign sugar
of crystallised tears.

The sky changes colour
like currency.
The music that is soft
from an excess of shadows
casts its threads of cotton
across an arena of yearning
and white teeth.

The edges of your language
fall back to you.
The doorways through which
the women disappear
give back to the world
a jungle of oranges
and a tide of warm water.

You feel that you can taste
the crushed powder of their lives
when you dry your face in a towel
that has been faded by the air
of a thousand burials and festivals.

But you can't see
into the shadows that live here
chained to their dances
and the clothes you leave behind.
You can't look into a fistful of clay
and see fixed ancient stars
in the purple seam of their unshakable night.

All you can have is your own dream
and a triumph of homelessness
under an orchestra of summer rain.

BLEAK HOUSE

The rain drags its small hands
down the window pane.
It brings word from the other side.
It says that the dead are still melancholic.
It says that they are nostalgic for this deep interior
varnished with tea and wine
like an old and self-important canvas.
I can see how they would be drawn
to this static world governed by poor light
and the patrician gaze of its trophies,
resigned, distant and courteous.

FARMERS

They were most at home
when the phantoms that visit
funerals and dances
dragged their tails
across the house
with tobacco smoke

The mist that clung
to the briars of their blood
had forsaken the sky
with the austerity of granite

Hating everyone who dreamed
they bullied the air
with their practical death
with the taut stupidity
of their seriousness

Wearing masks
swollen by the rain
they scattered with their eyes
the seeds of shame
on other peoples lives

PETITION

This road
touches
every dawn
dressed in an
elusive green
light
that has been
touched
by the sea

Under its
soft glance
you feel
the landscape's
sad petition
and from its
jungle of roots
the devastated
geometry
of its desire

Memories
older than
your years
ravage
your heart
with blades
of twisted smoke

ANCESTRAL MARCH

An unblemished yearning
triumphs over the dark waves
and the barbs of salt
that cling to my rough clothes.
Along this country road
a drunken ghost
dressed in a coat of barren weather
keeps me company.
The skirts of the waning light are beautiful.
Though the sky is a shroud
impressed with the stones
of countless cemeteries
it is also a veil
that makes heaven infinite and tender.
The sound and odour
of the sea water between the stones
hits home with the luxury of impenetrable blood.
Reaching me along the clandestine curve of twilight
the black water answers the questions of the sky
with an abiding sigh.

In Memory of My Father

My father is gone.
The house stares in through its own windows
as a crown of small hearts burns towards the roof.
His kind unshaven innocence drifts alone through everyone.
My mother turns to each newly arrived neighbour
referring to him as my darling
and our hearts are saddened further with love.
My mother, shocked now to realize through her tears,
through our tears, that she was really his lover,
tries to retain his tenderness
in the forsaken night of her new black clothes.
My father is gone, yet he is so near now,
in the rooms that are dense with subdued voices,
on the steps of the stairs,
through the telephone that continues to ring
asking if he is here.

SOME UNSPOKEN COMMITMENT

The fall comes
with its leaves and its learning.
Your elbows protrude
into the angelic evening
and the discipline
of the early night tells you
that the wind rattling your window
has something for you to do.

The swords
of wind and dying light
penetrate the trees
with an atrocity of hunger.
The implication of the rain
on the dark roofs
holds you by shame
to some unspoken commitment.

Fall arrives
an accessory to such immense sadness
that it pierces the hands of youth
with their own magic.
The hours pass
monumental as church pillars
obscuring the ritual.

SHRINE

Alcohol brings my blood
to a precipice of vapour
to the sky stretching
over the sea.
A foreboding thick as ivy
opens its fist in my throat.
The metallic light that falls
on the floor like straw
has the purity of a shrine.
Yet this burlesque is an affront
to the marble altars
that weigh on my eyes
because in this
dense migration of shadows
love gets confused with hunger.

VAINGLORIOUS

You are thinking of her as she sleeps
treacherously high above the streets.
The streets burn with the acid of crime
and the shy flame of desire.

You believe that she should want you
because you are a phantom
endowed with magnificent pain.

Thinking of her pulls the night together.
You know your heart could reveal to her
the remote and virtuous place
you believe she is homesick for.

You live inside a cave of absence
Your tortured world shivering with life
is your prize.

The alluring breeze that drives the clouds
tormented rapture is unfaithful.
The fickle rain wearing a virgins' blue gown
cannot dissolve your desire.

You believe that to hurt this much you must be blameless.
Moving through the placid night
you raise your voice and call to her
sleeping treacherously high above the streets.

BENEDICTION

Because we love
and pray our way
backwards and forwards
with the tides
when we finally touch
we find our defenceless
and hermitic tenderness
dressed in the smoke
of some vital benediction.
And because we know
that this is magic
we struggle to bring
to our open hands
the enigmatic love
of a magician's white birds.
And we learn
as we enter that place
between memory and prophecy
that the thing of desire
is the thing half hidden
it is a rush of horses
emanating from itself
crossing the tense bow
that is poised
above the rhythm of the sand.

DRAMA

You are lost
in this production
you have mounted.
You demand
to be watched
as you
deflect and encourage.
You know
the things you do
survive your absence
because you manoeuvre
the contours of love
so well.
Your light is sombre.
Your drama tragic
as you use the shell
of your savage jewellery
to protect
the implicit sweetness
of your breast.

BURDEN OF DESIRE

Your body conceals the night
with damp promises
wrapped in immaculate sheets.
You have censored the darkness
of everything
except its emblems
of longing and refuge.
You disguise yourself in pain
that can be so easily worn
letting every utterance
fall sweetly
into your burden
of silence and desire.
Your body suggests
it is the failure
of so many other nights
that brings the world
to your window
when finally you confide
the inevitable embrace
you pretended you would deny.

NIGHT TRAIN

I have paid my passage
but I have not departed.
I am thinking of your room
and how like a star
it is tied to the night.
I am thinking of you
a mother who has never
neglected her own breasts
allowing them to be nursed
by soft light
and shades of copper.
I have always leaned
towards the cold world
from some place warm
and towards somewhere warm
when my weariness was heavy
with rain and coffee.
This night can run
thin and blue along a steal rail
or fall towards
the lavish desolation
of your lips
poised in unfaithful tenderness.
The night is cold and abstract.
I know that your room
is abundant with perfume
and fragmented light
like buried treasure.
This night with you
will burn bright and die.
This night alone
will be buried
among all the others
like a playing card.

Fire and the Night

I feel strange among these people
who regard the streets as their own.
The naked trees
observing themselves beneath
the cold mercurial surface of the river
look lost
the way human things looked lost.
This is a foreign city.
This is a night wrongly accused.
This is autumn without a dream . . .
my girl is dead.
To be reconciled in the face of all that
would be to lie to myself successfully.
So maybe I will become a vagabond again
looking for grace
between my fire and the night
my food growing cold in the wind
and my sleep threatened.

HOUSES

The houses along this street
are strangers
even to each other.
They are oppressed by the taste
of their own hearts.
The trees
with the complicity of servants
fan their foolish dignity
which is laughable.
The windows are lakes
marked by the oily colours of the moon
where treachery and desire
have been held under
like unwanted children.

BLUE DRESS

The night bartered away in anger
could not be saved by music.
The moon at the end of the street
can attest to this.
The house was held in hands
the colour of alcohol and money.
Snarled roots haunted the rooms
and braided light covered the walls like water.
The night was calico blue
and she wore a blue dress
to suggest that she was leaving.
In the iris of her eye
he thought he saw her sweet insignia.
Listless she mounted her indolent protest.
Morning has arrived.
The distance between them is furious with leaves.

EMPTINESS AND WAITING

Far away there is rain in the mountains
and the river is deep and determined.
The house we lived in,
silent as a heart that has stopped beating,
waits to find its purpose in the snow.
I am forced to live again by befriending
the world on the street,
pursuing things I no longer want
because I am afraid of what I might see
if I allow myself to have no desire.
The future is lit by a naked bulb
and vacant as those neglected rooms
that float like ghosts above these city shops.
My strength seems only for waiting
for what I cannot tell.
I feel a terrible emptiness
not even sadness or the rain
or the wind coming off the ocean
can touch.

Arms of a Dancer

Persistent as daylight
weeds find a neglected place
and the dancing leaves
reckless and hesitant
brooding and frantic
trail their tiny gowns of sand
across your path.
Like dawn or twilight
like the tide
your flesh will not wait
so don't bully your own heart.
Quietly draw an oar
from your cross of light
and with the arms of a dancer
push away from this tarnished stone.
Your body beneath
the apathy of your dress
knows everything
it knows that it is good to want to be free
and that your hands
that have touched so many things
need to reach out and show
their own whiteness to the sky.

THE NIGHT

The night is being a mother to her stars.
Under the town's soft shell of light
    a hopeful sadness undulates like music.

The night is full of wings and damp paper.
Gently the river's breath reaches the streets
    as it flows with a slow heart towards winter.

The night whispers in the threads of its own burning oil.
Counters of zinc are pushed silently
    into a crypt of alcohol and cologne.

The night drifts in and out of rented rooms.
Behind the mist at the edge of town
    there is a solemn orchard of water and flesh.

The night rests on the world like a leaf.
In the eyes of those who do not sleep
    small kingdoms of ice and iron shine.

A New Era

I don't know my way around.
These faded streets surprise my heart
with the vapour of estrangement
and the charity of amber light.
There is a hole in the world
through which I pursue
my vocation of longing
and desperate affection.
In an intoxicating depth
that holds my spirit gently
all the sensations of life visit me
while all my actions look for justice
for having left home.
A new era is beginning,
though it hovers with a faint light
an inch above the cold ground
it keeps me conscious of the sky.
There is a new life to be filled in
among the fallen leaves
and the grey air between the houses.
Behind the fog
rivers quiet as serpents
wait to penetrate my dreams.

CAPRICIOUS REALM

To survive the multitude of lost evenings
I transform my wounds to look like stars.
I am king of my own capricious realm
as I make desperate excursions
to the end of every street.
I am infatuated with the night.
My sleeplessness reveals to me
the contours of a hidden world
a world that is lost,
a world of grandeur and archaic light.

FROM MY WINDOW

Like others who are drunk and poor
my room hinges on the street
drawing me to the window for company.
The street is decorated with wolves teeth
a scavengers' heart and a cry of untraceable rage.
The women act indifferent to its flamboyant overture.
They are alert to the dangerous odour of instinct.
Angry that they have to love anyone at all
they hide their beauty in an attitude of porcelain
dressed as stone.
The breeze sweeps their hearts with rain.
Ignoring the rain
they balance on a grid of reflected light
demonstrating how exotic they are
how indestructible they have become.
Yet something in them relents
as they consider the drift of their own cigarette smoke
and cautiously they offer their hands
as things that must be tamed
like a gift of birds or horses.

Waiting for Rain

These grey days
are suspended with sorrow.
I would prefer that it rained.
In the ceaseless
implications of the wind
I wait for my sadness
to find its meaning.
It is getting late.
Along this rough sidewalk
of packed snow
sleep pursues me
dressed as Death's
younger sister.
You are gone forever
and I am trapped
in something
more immense than life
that leaves me desolate
as the prayers that I condemn
to the crystals of cold air.
My heart has been thrown back
to a world
that absorbs and holds
so many shades
that have no colour.

LANCING STREET

The grey rain
searches the screens.
Lives fail.
When you are poor
Sunday is to be feared
as it assails you
with old dreams
that have thrown off
their grandeur.
On the pallid ledger
of the afternoon
an indifferent Jesus
writes in smoke.
The odours coming
from where other people live
smother the senses
with a fevered blanket
of potent weeds.
The children play.
A sphere of discord
rolls within them
stifling their hearts.

SLANDERED

She laughs because she is sad.
You see she is ugly
and has been slandered
by something scribbled
on the wall of the world.
Her eyes possess the sea and the clouds
confused in the distance.
Her ugliness she thinks
she sorcerously wished upon herself
but she feels
her sense of beauty
weighing like the sky
on her breast.
She knows her life is tragic
as a ship going down
so she lets the fire
of her forsaken heart
burn in its own honour.

LIGHT AND LOSS

Those who are lost
look so earnest
as they watch each day
rise up and divide like smoke.
In their enigmatic countenance
you can trace
the profile of something
that you have forgotten.
You can see in the temper
of their eyes
that the past
can never go away
that the sky is circular
like a prayer.
You become alarmed
to find yourself envying
their valour of soft stone
and how simply they own
the things that come to them
as they measure
their circumstance
by the drift of the rain
and by the sheaves of light
touching the world.

DEEP WATER

Have I imprisoned myself
in this city that is my enemy
doing time without ocean or lake
to give potency to my idleness.
This is a feast that offers no sustenance.
This is food consumed before an execution.
I cannot go on any longer
searching for the meaning of being lost.
This hard ground
won't let me at the root of my dreams.
I need the pliable earth.
I need the soft and gregarious shadows.
I need the good council
of deep and expansive water.

STONE BIRD

The city, staunch and indifferent
as a stone bird
watches a replica of passing time
drift by on the harbour floor

A spiral of young voices
playing at being reckless
rope in everything
unfulfilled in the distance

Their song is composed of missing ships
and the dream that drives it
is a searching light
whose source has already died

I Want to Leave this City

I want to leave this city
and go where the water and the sky
slowly pull the evening out of the trees.
I want to leave this city
so I can miss you properly.
Perfect memories
are always damp with faint new colours
that light up the heart like a smooth stone
at the door of a cave.
I want to miss you
and smell the earth under the spears of grass
like I used to pick up
on the promises and inevitabilities of your fragrance.
I want to miss you
and not get tempted to put anything right
just let everything burn like brave candles
at a recently abandoned table.

THE EBB AND FLOW

Every breath we take
is a remnant torn from the sea.
The waves are a congregation of lovers
breaking open their vows on the sand.
The smell of the sea holds
a certainty so deep
it has no path.
It crosses the furrows of the sand
with the prowess of rain
and the consolation of light.
It reaches us as an elaborate flora
that adheres to each kiss.
These end of summer days
cling to the world like rust to a blade.
A perennial wish
resting in the dry grass
shuffles with reminiscences.
The evenings are sinking ships
that stain the tide with oil and music.
Beneath the skirts of this ebbing season
the aroma of yearning
pursues the horizon forever.

THE PATHS WE TOOK TOGETHER

There are so many places
we walked together
that I can go on
remembering you forever.
I try to keep your voice
close to me
asking you for a sign
so I can understand a little
the context of this sphere.
The paths we took together
now hang wistfully
over the rivers and lakes
and under clouds
that anoint them
with the aura of an evening
that is lonelier than the world.
My heart jumps like water
under a sheaf of light
defining my position
beneath a sky
that no longer exists.
Through the evening dust
that rises gently
over the warm roads
I see my future
stretch out
sweet and melancholy
like a memory
where the communion of souls
is easily imagined.